SCIENCE Q&A

WEATHER

— Janice Parker —

Weigl Publishers Inc.

Published by Weigl Publishers Inc.
350 5th Avenue, 59th Floor
New York, NY 10118

Website: www.weigl.com

Library of Congress Cataloging-in-Publication Data

Parker, Janice.
  Weather : Science Q & A / Janice Parker.
       p. cm.
  Includes index.
  ISBN 978-1-59036-952-4 (hard cover : alk. paper) -- ISBN 978-1-59036-953-1 (soft cover : alk. paper)
  1. Weather--Juvenile literature. I. Title.
  QC981.3.P367 2009
  551.5--dc22
                              2008003891

Printed in the United States of America in North Mankato, Minnesota
2 3 4 5 6 7 8 9 0 13 12 11 10 09

122009
WEP17000

Project Coordinator
Heather Hudak

Design
Terry Paulhus

Photo credits

All images provided by Getty Images unless otherwise noted.

Yankee Publishing, Inc: page 7 bottom.

CONTENTS

What is weather?

Have you ever seen a tornado, had a sunburn, or watched your dog hide from a thunderclap? If so, you have experienced just three of the thousands of effects the weather can have on your life. Weather is caused by the conditions that exist in the air around you. It can be hot, cold, wet, or dry. It can be windy, calm, stormy, or **humid**.

All weather has four main ingredients. These are temperature, wind, water, and air pressure. We know a great deal about the science at work in making weather, but not enough to make weather predictable. Weather can change without warning. It can sometimes work silently, such as when the Sun's rays burn your skin, or it can make a grand entrance, as tornadoes and hurricanes do, leaving destruction in its path.

How did people forecast weather in the past?

For centuries, people have tried to learn about and forecast the weather. Throughout the world and throughout history, people have used many different methods of predicting the weather.

find it quick

Visit **http://teacher.scholastic.com/ activities/wwatch** to learn more about forecasting the weather.

undreds of years ago, people
Europe believed that animal
ehavior changed depending
n the weather. For example,
eople believed that
edgehogs could predict
e end of winter.

When European settlers
rrived in North America, they
ould not find hedgehogs, so they
ecided to use groundhogs instead.

ccording to tradition, groundhogs
nd their hibernation on February 2nd,
gnaling the end of winter. The tradition
ays that if a groundhog comes out of
e ground and sees its shadow, it gets
ightened and runs back into the
round. This means there will be six
ore weeks of winter. Scientists who
ave studied the groundhog theory have
oncluded that this traditional method
f forecasting weather does not work.

■ Punxsutawney Phil is a well-known
weather-predicting groundhog.

A tradition that has a history of success is
the Old Farmer's Almanac. First published
in 1792, the Old Farmer's Almanac gives
information about weather, the rise and
set of the Sun, and the tides. Its weather
forecasts are correct about 80 percent of
the time—a very good rate. The forecasts
are given on the basis of weather
folklore and a secret scientific formula.
Many farmers and other people whose
jobs depend on the weather rely on the
advice in the Old Farmer's Almanac.

I spy

The Old Farmer's Almanac is so accurate
that the United States government almost
prevented it from being published during
World War II. In 1942, a German spy was caught
by officials on Long Island, New York. The spy
had a copy of the Old Farmer's Almanac in his
pocket. The government was worried that the publication could
supply the enemy with important information. In the end, it was
decided that the almanac could continue to be published.

How is temperature measured?

Everyone can tell the difference between hot and cold. Often, however, it important to know exactly how hot or how cold something is.

...mperature is measured by ...ermometers. Scientists in the 17th ...ntury realized that water always boils ...d freezes at the same temperatures. ...is discovery helped scientists make a ...mperature scale. The scale allowed all ...ientists to measure temperature with ...e same numbers.

...e German scientist, Gabriel Fahrenheit, ...as the first person to use mercury in ...ermometers. Mercury responds quickly ...temperature changes, swelling when it ...ts warmer and shrinking ...hen it gets colder. ...hrenheit made a ...mperature scale that ...still used today in the ...nited States. He set 0° ...hrenheit as the lowest ...inter temperature where he ...ed in Germany.

...1742, Anders Celsius, a Swedish ...tronomer, developed a scale with ...mpler numbers. He made the freezing ...int of water 0°C and the boiling

point 100°C. His system is used today, especially by scientists, who find the system easier to use than the Fahrenheit method. Most countries in the world have also adopted the Celsius system. The United States is one of the only countries still using the Fahrenheit system.

■ Mercury, also known as quicksilver, can be very dangerous to human health. Most thermometers today use other substances to measure temperature.

Revolution

Galileo Galilei is credited with inventing the thermometer in the 1590s. Galileo also built the first effective telescope and used it to prove that Earth revolves around the Sun.

What is the Sun?

The Sun rises and sets everyday. It is always sunny somewhere on Earth. The Sun gives us warmth and light. What else does the Sun do for Earth?

The Sun is about 4.5 billion years old. Scientists believe there has been life on Earth for about 5 billion years.

The Sun is the key to life on Earth. Without the Sun, the planet would freeze, and all life that relies on its energy for growth and food would die. People who lived in ancient times worshiped the Sun. They knew of its great importance in maintaining life on Earth. However, they did not understand the science behind the Sun's power. We now understand some of the ways the Sun's energy influences weather. Everything from wind to temperature is affected by the Sun.

The Sun is a giant ball of fiery gases 93 million miles (150 million kilometers) away from Earth. It is our closest star and one of the hundred billion stars in our galaxy.

The Sun sends out large amounts of energy in all directions. Only about two-billionths of the total output reach Earth. This is enough energy to provide plenty of light and heat for all the plants and animals on Earth. Without the Sun's energy, the temperature on Earth would be no higher than -418° Fahrenheit (-250° Celsius).

The Sun's energy arrives on Earth as different types of radiant energy, or rays. Although you cannot see **infrared** rays, you can feel them. When infrared rays hit your skin, or any other object, the energy usually turns into heat. Nearly all of the heat on Earth comes from the infrared rays of sunshine.

Hot enough for you?

The temperature on the surface of the Sun is 10.832° Fahrenheit (6,000°C). The Sun's core reaches a temperature of about 27,000,000°F (15,000,000°C).

What happens when sunlight reaches Earth?

When the Sun's rays reach Earth, the energy may be absorbed by land, water, or air. In each case, the results are quite different.

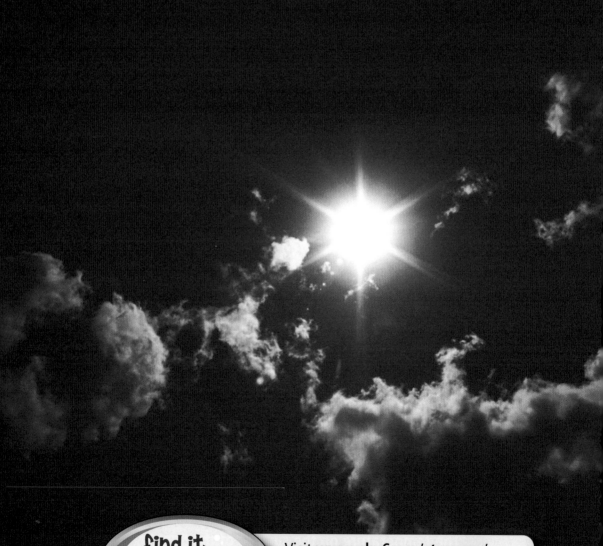

find it quick

Visit **www.phy6.org/stargaze/ Sun1lite.htm** to learn more about how the Sun affects Earth.

r absorbs some of the Sun's energy as e rays pass through, but most of the ys move through the air until they ach water or land.

nd features such as soil, rocks, and vement become warm when they sorb the Sun's energy. As the mperature of the land rises, some the heat is given off into the air se to the ground. This makes the

■ Water vapor that remains close to the ground is called mist.

air temperature rise. Then, when the air moves, it carries the heat from one place to another.

When water absorbs sunrays, the energy causes some of the water to evaporate, or turn into gas, and enter the air as water vapor. This creates humidity and clouds.

Warm waters

Water can absorb a great deal of heat without showing much of an increase in temperature. Land that is near oceans and large lakes does not become as warm as land that is far from bodies of water. However, water also holds onto its heat energy longer than land does. For this reason, coastal cities stay warmer in the winter than inland cities.

Why do the seasons change

Everyone on Earth experiences changing seasons. In some places, the difference between winter and summer can be drastic, from sunshine and hot temperatures to snow and ice. Other places experience less noticeab changes, perhaps only a few degrees.

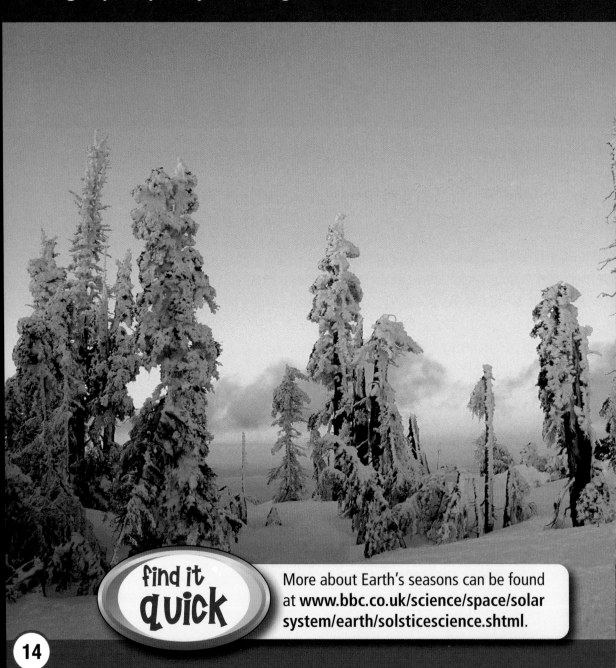

find it quick

More about Earth's seasons can be found at **www.bbc.co.uk/science/space/solar system/earth/solsticescience.shtml**.

asons are caused when different nounts of the Sun's energy reach Earth different times of the year. Earth's **axis** tilted as it makes its yearlong **orbit** ound the Sun. When it is summer in e Northern Hemisphere, the Sun's ys strike the top half of Earth directly.

At the same time, the rays reaching the Southern Hemisphere are more indirect. They cover a much larger area, so the region is cooler. During the spring and autumn, the Sun is most direct at the **equator**.

Here is your challenge!

Create a model of the Sun as it would be seen from space. Use this model to track how the Sun moves across the sky in one 24-hour period.

1. Draw an "X" in the center of a sheet of white paper. Then, place the paper on a flat surface outdoors. Be sure that the paper is in a place where there is sunlight for the entire day.
2. Place a clear plastic bowl upside down over the "X" on the piece of paper. Next, mark the bottom of the bowl with an "X." Be sure the "X" on the paper is in line with the "X" on the bowl. Now, use a pencil to trace the outer edge of the bowl onto the paper.
3. Use a compass to locate north, and mark this spot on the paper.
4. Every hour, place the pencil on the outside of the bowl so that the shadow of the point lines up with the "X" on the paper. Mark the location with a small circle, and label it with the time of day. Repeat this step for several hours.

Can you predict where the next small circle will be placed? Which direction is the Sun moving?

What is the greenhouse effect?

The "greenhouse effect" is the popular term for how the atmosphere he[lps] warm the global **ecosystem**. Just as glass on a greenhouse holds the Su[n's] warmth inside, so the atmosphere traps heat near Earth's surface and keeps Earth warm. The greenhouse effect makes Earth a good planet for living things.

find it quick

For more information about climate change and global warming, surf to **www.epa.gov/climatechange/kids**.

Air travel is a leading cause of the greenhouse effect. Many people who travel on airplanes day donate money to environmental causes to offset their impact on the environment.

s a natural part of Earth's greenhouse fect, the planet periodically warms and ools. Some people are concerned about e present warming trend because it is appening faster than ever before. any human activities are adding reenhouse gases such as carbon oxide and methane to the atmosphere. ctivities that produce these gases clude farming, mining coal, and ving airplanes.

We cannot be sure how global warming will affect us in the future. If greenhouse gases in the atmosphere increase, global temperatures might rise to a level that could become very dangerous. If Earth's water warms and expands, polar ice and **glaciers** may melt. Some coastal areas may be permanently flooded, and people could lose their homes. Changing temperatures could also affect crop growth, causing food shortages in some areas.

Slow down

The average car gives off more than its own weight in carbon dioxide each year. Driving fast burns more fuel and causes more pollution than driving slowly for the same distance.

When are the Sun's rays deadly?

Some of the Sun's energy is necessary for life, but too much can be harm

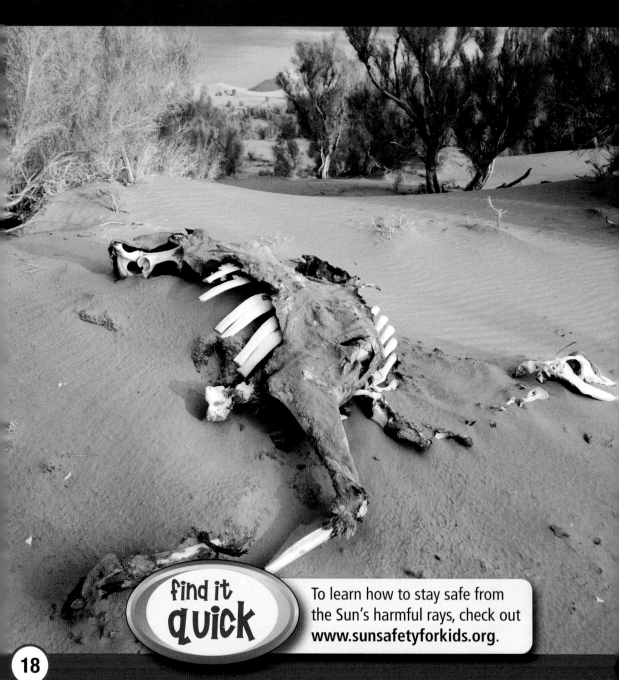

find it quick

To learn how to stay safe from the Sun's harmful rays, check out **www.sunsafetyforkids.org**.

traviolet (UV) rays from the
n can cause skin cancer,
cluding the deadly form known
melanoma. Other effects of UV
ys include damaged eyesight
d, possibly, weaker defenses
ainst infection. The United
ates has estimated that every
e percent of **ozone** loss causes
ousands more cases of skin
ncer each year, and blindness
100,000 people worldwide.
traviolet radiation also harms
ater animals such as plankton,
ellfish, and fish. Too much UV
nlight has caused sheep to go
ind in southern Chile. Some
g species could be at risk
extinction because UV rays
mage their eggs. Crops grow
aller leaves if UV rays increase.
is harms food production.

■ Metastatic is a rare type
of skin cancer, but it causes
most skin cancer deaths.

Sun is shining

Sunburns and suntans are caused by
two different types of UV rays. A sunburn
may become lighter as it heals, but it will
never become a suntan.

What makes the wind blow?

Wind is the movement of air. Sometimes, air moves so fast that it knocks over buildings. On a very calm day, it might feel like there is no wind at a

find it quick

Explore **www.weatherwiz kids.com/wind1.htm** to learn more about the wind.

arth is surrounded by a blanket of air lled the atmosphere. The atmosphere about 186 miles (300 km) thick. This ay seem very thick, but compared to arth's size, the atmosphere is like the in on an apple. The atmosphere gets inner on its outer edges. This means ere are fewer particles of air higher the atmosphere than ere are closer to arth's surface.

he wind blows for e same reason that ot-air balloons rise. ir moves, and heat es up.

round that is warmed the Sun transfers eat to the air. Air olecules move faster hen they are heated, umping into each ther more forcefully. he energetic molecules ush one another apart, d the air becomes inner and lighter.

Air will always move from areas where there are many air molecules to areas where there are few. The light air rises like a bubble. At the same time, heavier, cooler air moves in below to take its place. This causes the air to circulate. The basic rule is that whenever warm air and cool air meet, the wind will blow.

DAY

Warm air rises from the land.

Cool air moves in to take its place.

NIGHT

Cool air moves in to take its place.

Warm air rises from the ocean.

Dust in the wind

Scientists have found that wind can carry dust to North America from places as far away as Africa and China.

How is wind measured?

Much like measuring temperature, the measurement of wind speed and direction is very important. Farmers, pilots, and architects all need to kn○ wind patterns and speeds in order to do their jobs.

Wind vanes, also called weather vanes, are used to tell wind direction. As wind hits the side of a weather vane, the vane is pushed around so that it points into the wind. Airports often use wind socks made of cloth to show wind direction and speed. The socks fill with air and point in the direction the wind is blowing. Today's weather forecasters measure wind speed with an instrument called an anemometer. Most anemometers have several cups that spin when the wind blows. The anemometer counts how often the cups spin around the center. This number tells forecasters how fast the wind is blowing.

You can tell how fast wind is blowing even without instruments. By observing the movements of flags, people, trees, and other objects outside, it is easy to see the difference between a strong wind and a light wind.

■ Weather forecasters use anemometers to measure both wind speed and wind pressure.

Here is your challenge!

Which way is the wind blowing where you live? Make your own weather vane to find out.

1. Stick a pencil in a large lump of clay with the eraser end up. Be sure the pencil is steady.
2. Stick an arrowhead and tail made from cardboard in each end of a drinking straw.
3. Pin the straw onto the eraser.
4. Mark North, South, East, and West on the clay, and use a compass to position the wind vane on the wall of a fence.
5. Watch the vane turn in the wind. In which direction is the wind blowing?

What are air currents?

Wind blows around the world in set patterns. There are many elements that affect the way wind blows.

Imagine Earth is a big, smooth ball of oil, with no water or mountains. Now imagine that it stops rotating. If Earth were like this, the land at the equator would get the most heat, and air currents would always be the same. The heated air would rise and pull cooler air from both the north and south. When air rises, it expands because the pressure is lower at higher altitudes. Expanding air cools. The cooling air above ground would flow both north and south from the equator, then sink down, pushing the air below toward the equator. Air would form regular loops from the equator to the poles. Wind would always blow north and south from the poles to the equator.

Earth's rotation disturbs these ideal patterns. The air sinks to the surface before reaching the poles, causing trade winds to blow. The same thing happens when cold air moves from the poles. More than one "loop" of air helps make the world's air currents. Lakes, oceans, prairies, and mountains also disturb the smooth flow of air.

Polar easterlies
Polar front
Prevailing westerlies
Horse latitudes
Northeast trade winds
Doldrums
Southeast trade winds
Horse latitudes
Prevailing westerlies
Polar front
Polar easterlies

We shall prevail

In some areas, winds follow a regular pattern. The direction the wind blows from most often is called the "prevailing wind." These winds can deform the growth of trees.

What turns wind into a twister?

Tornadoes can happen during severe thunderstorms. Only one thundersto
in 1,000 produces a tornado. Winds in a tornado can reach 150 to 200 mi
(240 to 320 km) per hour.

Tornadoes can appear in many shapes and sizes. However, most appear in the form of a funnel.

Many tornadoes never touch the ground, but those that do suck up dirt, debris, and other objects. Tornadoes can even lift cars off the ground and completely destroy houses and other buildings. Roughly 1,000 tornadoes occur in North America every year.

Wild winds form inside thunderclouds as warm air moves in below cool air that is moving in a different direction.

Winds higher up in the cloud blow faster and in a different direction than winds below. The air begins to spin. As the air spins faster and faster, it becomes a column.

The funnel of spinning air pushes down through the cloud toward the ground. This is how a tornado forms.

Dark alley

The states of Texas, Kansas, Oklahoma, Nebraska, and Missouri are known as "Tornado Alley." These states have more tornadoes than anywhere else on Earth—more than 700 each year.

What is El Niño?

Natural disasters can be caused by events happening both inside and around our planet. One event has been blamed for many different disasters all over the world.

find it quick

Learn more about El Niño by finding it in the Weather Encyclopedia at **www.theweather channelkids.com/weatherED**.

arly Spanish sailors noticed periodic
hanges in water temperatures where
ey fished off the west coast of South
merica. They called the rise in
mperature El Niño, meaning "Christ
hild," because it always happened just
ter Christmas. The change happened
bout once every seven years.

ru's cool coastal waters normally
ave some of the best fishing areas
the world. During El Niño, however,
change in wind patterns causes the
ater to warm. The ocean currents
ange, and the best fishing waters
rface far from shore.

■ Landslides and other changes caused by
El Niño cause thousands of deaths and billion
of dollars in damage.

The shifting patterns of El Niño have
many other effects. There are changes in
temperature and wind patterns around
the world. El Niño has been blamed for
everything from droughts in Africa and
Australia, to floods in Ecuador, and
landslides in California. Some people
believe it has even caused outbreaks
of tropical diseases.

Look on the bright side

El Niño is not all bad. Researchers have found that El Niño
reduces the number of hurricanes developing in the Atlantic
Ocean and the number of tornadoes in the central United States.

How does water affect the weather?

Without water, there would be no weather. Water vapor in the air interac
with heat from the Sun to create weather patterns on Earth.

Dew forms when surfaces near the ground become cool enough for water vapor in the air to condense. When warm, moist air reaches the temperature at which it cannot hold water in a gas form, beads of water appear on the surface.

eather only happens in the region of e atmosphere that is about 6 miles 0 km) above Earth. This region is called e troposphere. Only the troposphere ntains water that has been evaporated om Earth's surface.

ater vapor is invisible, but even on bright, clear, cloudless day, there is ater vapor in the air. When the Sun ines on oceans, lakes, rivers, and nds, it always causes some water to aporate. Evaporation means that water turns from a liquid that people can see into a gas that cannot be seen.

There is a limit to the amount of water vapor that the air can hold. If you try to add more, some of the vapor will condense, or turn into liquid. The temperature of the air determines how much water it can hold. Warm air holds much more water than cold air. For example, air at 86° Fahrenheit (30°C) can hold more than six times as much water vapor as air at 32° Fahrenheit (0°C).

Vaporized

The air in your lungs holds as much water vapor as possible. The water vapor is the same temperature as your body—98.6° Fahrenheit (37°C). When you breathe out in the winter, the warm air from your body combines with cold air that cannot hold as much water vapor. When you "see" your breath, some of the water vapor has condensed into tiny droplets of water.

How do clouds form?

Clouds can be big and fluffy or thin and wispy. They can make rain or off
shade. They can take many different shapes. How are clouds made?

find it quick

Find out more about clouds at
www.weatherwizkids.com/cloud.htm.

People can predict the weather based on the type of cloud they see.

Clouds are made of tiny droplets of water or ice crystals in the air. When warm, moist air meets cooler air, some warm air cools and cannot hold all of its water vapor. Some of the extra water changes into a liquid or even freezes. This forms clouds.

Clouds come in a variety of sizes and shapes. Most clouds belong to one of three basic categories—cumulus, stratus, or cirrus. You may also see the word "nimbus" added to a cloud name. For example, a cumulonimbus cloud is a rain cloud.

Cumulus clouds are puffy with flat bottoms. These clouds can be as high as 14,000 feet (4,267 meters) in the air. Cumulus clouds often form on warm summer days and then disappear at night.

Cirrus clouds are made of ice crystals. They form very high in the sky, usually above 25,000 feet (7,620 m). Cirrus clouds have a wispy, feathery appearance. The winds blow cirrus clouds into fine strands that are sometimes called "mares' tails."

Stratus clouds form quite low and often cover the sky like a gray sheet. The clouds barely move, and the air under them is very still. These conditions can make the sky look dull and heavy.

Get cirrus

Airplanes make cirrus clouds when water vapor from their engines forms ice crystals. The clouds look like long streaks high in the sky.

What causes rain?

We know that clouds are made of water, so why are not all clouds rain clouds?

cloud droplet has a million times less
ater than a typical raindrop. Cloud
oplets are very light and tiny. Stormy
r in the sky tosses small droplets
ound so much that they usually cannot
ll to the ground. They will not fall until
ey collide with each other and join
gether to make larger, heavier droplets.

the air is very still, smaller drops may
ll to the ground as the form of rain
lled drizzle. Larger raindrops usually
art as ice crystals near the center of
mulus clouds. The ice crystals collect
ater from droplets in the clouds. The
ystals grow larger and larger until they
e heavy enough to fall through the

■ Drops of water more than 0.02 inches (0.05
centimeters) in size are rain. Smaller drops are
called drizzle.

turbulent air. While passing through
warm air close to Earth, the crystals melt
and turn into raindrops. If the air
temperature remains cold, the ice crystals
do not melt. They fall as snow.

During a severe storm, air currents may
push upward so violently that they carry
growing ice crystals and pellets high into
the clouds. Water continues to condense
on the crystals until they grow very large.
When the ice balls finally fall through the
warmer air below, they are too big to
completely melt. They fall as hailstones.

Drops of rain

Raindrops are shaped like disks, not teardrops. Raindrops are
round when they leave the clouds, but the wind resistance, or
pressure, on the way to Earth flattens them slightly.

What is a thunderstorm?

A thunderstorm has very violent winds, thunder, and lightning. Clouds m
rise as high as 14 miles (22 km). The energy of a thunderstorm is much
greater than the energy of an atomic bomb.

find it quick

Try controlling the weather in a
virtual environment at
www.scholastic.com/kids/weather.

Mountain ranges can create interesting weather patterns. Often, one side of a mountain range will experience wet, rainy weather, while the other side will experience dry conditions.

Thunderstorms often occur after a long period of hot weather. This is because the ground becomes very warm from the heat of the Sun.

A thunderstorm begins when drafts of warm air move upward, creating a large cumulus cloud. When the cloud is high enough for the rain to begin, the thunderstorm is mature. As rain falls through the cloud, it cools the air, causing **downdrafts**. The air in the cloud becomes very turbulent. Finally, the rain cools all of the air in the cloud until there are no more **updrafts**. The rain stops, and winds scatter the cloud.

Look up...look way up

You can tell whether a thunderstorm or just rain is coming by looking at clouds in the distance. Tall clouds mean a thunderstorm is on the way. Thinner clouds will bring a slower and steadier rain.

What causes lightning and thunder?

Thunder and lightning can be dangerous, frightening, or beautiful. Something special must happen in the sky to create so much energy.

ce particles and
raindrops in clouds
are made of molecules.
Collisions between ice
particles and raindrops
break negatively charged
particles, called electrons,
off their molecules. When
a particle loses electrons,
it becomes positively
charged. These positively
charged particles cause
nearby particles to
become negatively
charged. Positive charges
collect in the top part of
the thundercloud, while
clusters of negative charges collect
at the bottom. The ground becomes
charged as well. Opposite charges
attract each other with such a strong
force that the charges leap from
cloud to cloud or between clouds
and the ground. This giant electric
spark is lightning.

When lightning strikes, it instantly
heats the air. The quick expansion of
the warm air starts a shock wave that
is heard as thunder. Lightning and
thunder happen at the same time,
but thunder is heard later because
light travels faster than sound.

Positive charge
Negative charge
Air currents move upward.
Air currents move downward.

Here is your challenge!

Step 1. Tear a sheet of paper into small pieces, like confetti.
Step 2. Hold a comb close to the bits of paper.
Step 3. Run the comb through your hair.
Step 4. Repeat step 2.

You have created static electricity. This is the same type of electricity as a lightning bolt.

What causes a hurricane?

A hurricane is a powerful storm that can destroy entire cities with wind and rain. A storm can officially be called a hurricane when its wind speed reaches 75 miles (121 km) per hour. Hurricanes cause billions of dollars in damage and kill thousands of people every year.

find it quick

Visit **http://eo.ucar.edu/webweather** to learn how hurricanes form and other interesting weather facts.

hurricane happens when air currents
ear the equator begin to circulate, and
everal thunderstorms are pulled
gether. Updrafts of warm, moist
r form storm clouds, and the rain
egins. The condensation of the water
eases energy to strengthen the
drafts. At the top, the air moves
t and begins to drop. Near the
rface of the ocean, the air is drawn
ck toward the center. The air picks
more moisture from the warm ocean
d creates more updrafts. The cycle
ntinues, and the storm grows.

■ Hurricanes cause huge, powerful waves to crash into the shore. This causes the shoreline to be washed away, or eroded. Erosion can cause entire buildings to collapse into the ocean, because the ground below the buildings is washed away.

As long as the hurricane is over water, it can maintain or increase its strength. When it moves onto land, it causes enormous damage to lives and to property in its path. When it runs out of water, the hurricane loses energy and dies out.

Thundering typhoons

Hurricanes only originate in the Atlantic Ocean. Powerful storms that originate in the Pacific Ocean are called typhoons.

Why is fresh water important?

Earth is often called the "water planet" because about 70 percent of its surface is covered with water. However, less than three percent of all the world's water is fresh, drinkable, and accessible.

ith such a limited supply of fresh water, weather disaster such as a drought can use serious problems. For example, the ississippi River is the United States' ost important inland route for ansporting products by boat. Inland arges and tugboats carry their cargoes ore than 1,800 miles (2,900 km) south the Gulf of Mexico. In 1988, a severe ought dried up so much of the river at boat traffic had to stop.

In desperation, the state of Illinois decided it could increase the amount of water in the river by draining water from Lake Michigan and Lake Huron, two of the five Great Lakes. These lakes contain almost one-fifth of the entire world's fresh water. Other states that border Lake Michigan and Lake Huron objected to the plan, and so did the government of Canada. In the end, the drainage plan was abandoned.

Droughts can cause many problems for people in affected regions. Along with water shortages, ese include death of livestock, fewer crops, wildfires, and desertification. Desertification is when area becomes so dry it turns into a desert.

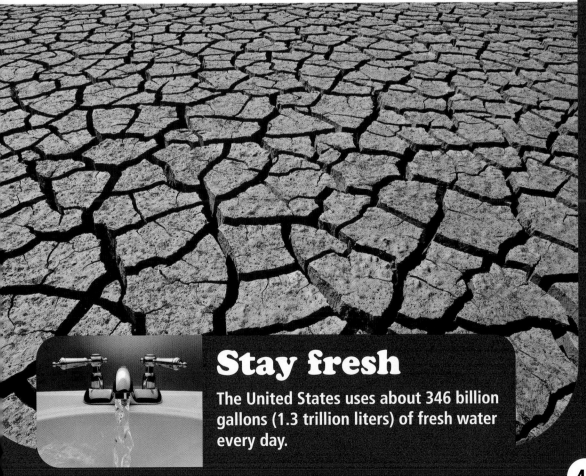

Stay fresh

The United States uses about 346 billion gallons (1.3 trillion liters) of fresh water every day.

Weather Careers

Meteorologist

Meteorologists use technology such as computers, **satellites**, and **radar** to help them forecast the weather. They tell people what the day-to-day weather is and what can be expected for the next few months. They also warn people about dangerous weather systems, such as tornadoes and hurricanes.

Meteorologists research ways to prevent weather that is dangerous to humans. This includes **seeding** clouds before they become violent storms. Most meteorologists work in government offices and have degrees in meteorology.

Storm Chaser

Some people try to get as close as possible to tornadoes. These "tornado hunters" or "storm chasers" are well trained in tornado safety.

Storm chasers listen to weather reports for clues about where a tornado might happen. If a tornado appears, the storm chasers have special equipment that will help them observe the storm. Video cameras record the tornado, while other machines measure the temperature, wind speed, and air pressure inside the tornado. The information they collect is given to scientists who study tornadoes.

find it **quick**

To learn about other weather careers, visit **www.mscd.edu/~career/meteor.htm**.

Young scientists at work
Test Your Knowledge

Test your weather knowledge with these questions and activities. You can probably answer the questions using only this book, your own experiences, and your common sense.

Fact:
Coastal areas have warmer summers and milder winters than inland areas.

Test:
You can do an experiment to show how water affects temperature. Place an empty glass and a glass full of water in the refrigerator. Wait 15 minutes. Then take the glasses out of the refrigerator. Which glass feels warmer? Look back to page 13 to find out why.

Fact:
One of the best ways to measure wind speed is by observing the effects of wind. Admiral Francis Beaufort designed a wind scale in the 1800s to help sailors judge wind speed. Today's Beaufort scale has been adapted for use on land.

Test:
Match the pictures to the appropriate wind speeds from the Beaufort scale.

A. less than 1 mph (1.6 kph)   D. 47–54 mph (76–87 kph)
B. 8–12 mph (13–19 kph)   E. more than 75 mph (121 kph)
C. 25–31 mph (40–50 kph)

1   2   3   4   5

Answers: 1. C, 2. B, 3. A, 4. D, 5. E

Take a weather survey

Are you prepared for a weather emergency? The American Red Cross and The Weather Channel conducted a survey of 2,039 Americans, aged 18 or older. They were asked a variety of questions to find out how prepared people are in case of a weather-related disaster, such as a flood, blizzard, hurricane, or tornado.

Do you believe that a weather-related disaster like a flood or hurricane could happen where you live?

Would you and your family be prepared if a weather emergency happened right now?

Have you and your family prepared an emergency supply kit to get you through a weather disaster?

Have you and your family ever practiced what to do in case of an emergency?

Would you know what to do and where to go if you were told to evacuate your home?

Do you or any family members have first-aid training?

Survey Results: Nearly every day, reporters and news broadcasters cover stories about weather-related disasters such as droughts, heat waves, cold snaps, tornadoes, and floods.

More than half of the people surveyed believed that a weather-related disaster was unlikely to happen where they live. Only one in six people believed such an event was very likely to happen. Only one in seven people said they would be completely prepared if a weather emergency were to happen right now.